Focus on Feelings

© Play Therapy with Carmen

Increasing Emotional Literacy

Carmen Jimenez-Pride

MSW, LCSW, LISW-CP, SAP, RYT, RCYT, RPT-S

ABOUT THE AUTHOR

Carmen Jimenez-Pride, creator of Focus on Feelings® is a License Clinical Social Worker and Registered Play Therapist Supervisor, Certified EMDR Therapist, Internal Family Systems Therapist. She is an international speaker, award winning best-selling author and business consultant.

Carmen Jimenez-Pride is also the founder of Diversity in Play Therapy Inc. and the host of the Diversity in Play Therapy Summit.

Contact: **www.carmenpride.com**

Email: **Carmen@outspokenllc.com**

ANXIOUS

ASHAMED

BORED

BRAVE

CALM

CHILL

CONFIDENT

CONFUSED

CURIOUS

DISAPPOINTED

EMBARRASED

EXCITED

FOCUSED

FRUSTRATED

HAPPINESS

HOPELESS

HURT

IGNORED

IRRITATED

JEALOUS

MAD

OVERWHELMED

PLAYFUL

PROUD

REJECTED

SAD

SCARED

SHY

SNEAKY

UGH